MEANING OF PASSIVE INCOME

Passive earnings are money you earn that doesn't require you to do much work active" work to hold making it. In essence, you could do most of the work upfront and put in some additional effort to keep the income coming.

For instance, if you create a web path, you simply need to update its content to maintain the money flowing.

You've possibly heard the expression "make money while you sleep." That's the most important draw that entices people to earn passive profits.

You can create something (a blog, path, e-book, videos, or an internet store) that generates money even when you're not operating. Or you can make passive income investments (property or shares) that let you earn passively. (We'll let you know extra methods to earn like this quickly.)

Active profits vs. Passive Income: Which is excellent for me?

In idea, all of your income resources bring similar weight. But in relation to attaining financial freedom, passive earnings leaves energetic income within the dust.

You see, active income is the money generated from all those efforts you're currently making. And you want to preserve working in case you need to preserve making a residing. If you give up, you don't receives a commission. Your time actually equals money.

And you then have passive profits. An income that doesn't require you to work actively. And the money maintains to waft in for years and years. If you're trying to layout dream lifestyles wherein you are financially loose, it is probably higher so that it will cognizance on passive income.

Just remember, even as you is probably able to build a passive earnings stream with a small investment, you're now not making any much less of a dedication than a person investing their time. Making passive earnings comparable to profits earned from lively efforts calls for a terrific quantity of work prematurely.

23 GUIDELINES THAT CAN HELP YOU BECOME SUCCESSFUL THROUGH PASSIVE INCOME

1. Adventure Into dropshipping store

Dropshipping is one of the maximum worthwhile passive earnings assets. With dropshipping, you may discover trending products on marketplaces like AliExpress to promote to clients around the world. You can fill your on-line save with gadgets from numerous dropshipping niches, inclusive of style, domestic décor, or splendor.

The magic of dropshipping is that you construct your personal business and determine how an awful lot you rate for the products. In fact, from all of the passive earnings ideas on this listing, dropshipping is the only wherein you have got the most control over your margins.

You can sign up for Shopify to begin dropshipping nowadays. Once you create an internet keep, set up one of these dropshipping apps to find remarkable products to sell.

Note: A close alternative to a dropshipping store—but with loads extra enter into product choice and best control—is buying wholesale merchandise to promote on your keep. Using a wholesale market, you may connect to neighborhood US-based totally providers, buy products at wholesale fees, and sell them on in your target market. You can even integrate this selection with dropshipping by way of locating wholesalers who are willing to send merchandise directly for your customers.

2. Blogging

Another popular passive profits flow originates from blogging. Blogging has helped countless entrepreneurs earn passively through affiliate hyperlinks, guides, subsidized posts, merchandise, ebook offers, and many others.

It can indeed take quite a piece of upfront work to build a a success weblog. However, it's one of the most sustainable ways to generate an target audience through organic and social site visitors or building an e-mail listing. The biggest perk of getting a blog is that you could turn that one asset into several one of a kind streams of income.

So, in case you're seeking out an easy passive profits concept, blogging might be the right choice for you.

Desirae Odjick, founding father of Half Banked, explains, "I began my weblog to make talking about personal finance extra approachable, and as part of that, I have a tendency to percentage a lot of personal memories. They regularly blanketed shout-outs to the gear I become the usage of and found beneficial, so it was a herbal transition to feature associate hyperlinks as I joined the ones agencies' packages.

"Now that I've been overlaying non-public finance for nearly four years on my blog, the ones links reliably carry in four figures every month, as people discover my articles and begin to get their budget so as—and I sense great recommending them, because I do individually use all of my affiliate products. It's a notable manner to feature passive earnings on your enterprise, mainly in case you don't have passive products of your personal to promote … but!"

3. Selling of online courses

If you're an professional in a few problem or subject, selling online courses may be a superb passive income concept for you. Whether you sell them thru your personal website or online getting to know platforms like Udemy, you'll locate masses of those who are inclined to pay to get right of entry to your content.

Of course, matters are easier in case you promote on systems like Udemy, however your route can be closely discounted all through positive periods. This will have an effect on how plenty passive earnings you earn. In comparison, promoting thru your personal internet site gives you control over pricing, which means you don't ought to sacrifice your margins simply due to the fact others are promoting at a discounted price.

Sumit Bansal, founding father of TrumpExcel says, "I began a weblog approximately Excel spreadsheets in 2013. I did it as I was learning plenty approximately spreadsheets and idea it'd be a great way to percentage my information with others. It slowly started out getting traction in two years; it became getting a hundred,000+ page perspectives a month. I determined to create an online direction and see if it would fly, and it did. I made a great aspect income for some months and then determined to do this full time and launch extra courses. Since then, the weblog has grown lots, and I have been featured on many outstanding web sites and publications consisting of Prolonger, Your Story, Glass Door, CEO Magazine, etc."

4. Publish Instagram sponsored posts

If you've got fans on Instagram, you might want to try your hand at developing sponsored content material. Instagram backed posts are content material pieces that endorse a selected service or product (typically owned by the sponsoring birthday celebration). Sponsors compensate publishers for developing and distributing content that promotes their business.

The mystery to getting backed is to get more Instagram followers. You'll also want to be extremely good constant with the kind of content you publish so sponsors recognize what to anticipate. And make certain to focus on simply one area of interest—brands decide on creators who can post first-rate content material round a particular subject matter.

When it comes for your Instagram bio, make certain to feature your electronic mail deal with. As your account grows, you could lease virtual assistants to create sponsored posts on your behalf. The more subsidized submit requests you get, the more passive income you will be able to generate.

Sumit Bansal, founder of TrumpExcel says, "I started a blog approximately Excel spreadsheets in 2013. I did it as I was getting to know loads approximately spreadsheets and notion it might be a very good manner to share my information with others. It slowly commenced getting traction in years; it turned into getting a hundred,000+ page perspectives a month. I determined to create an internet path and notice if it'd fly, and it did. I made a terrific side profits for some months and then decided to try this complete time and release more guides. Since then, the weblog has grown a lot, and I have been featured on many distinguished web sites and guides which includes Prolonger, Your Story, Glass Door, CEO Magazine, and so forth."

5. Develop a print-on-demand store

With ecommerce being one of the maximum popular approaches to make passive income online, it most effective makes feel to give a shout-out to print on call for.

Print on demand lets in you to sell your custom pix on products like t-shirts, garb, mugs, canvases, smartphone cases, luggage, and extra. The high-quality issue approximately this is that you may build your personal branded products.

The only drawback is that you need to be savvy at picture design, due to the fact the margins are frequently too thin to outsource the designs cost effectively. However, if you create that unique triumphing design, your sales will take off. Plus, it's now not a extraordinary competitive enterprise, when you consider that other manufacturers are unlikely to promote the equal designs. Don't hesitate to start right away with Shopify!

How worthwhile is print on demand? Find the answer in our collaboration with Wholesale Ted, where we compare dropshipping with print on demand.

Veronica Wong, the founder of Boba Love, stocks how her love of bubble tea helped her earn passive earnings: "I've been drinking bubble tea for so long as I can do not forget, so combining my love for boba with my love for design appeared like a really perfect suit. I commenced designing and promoting bubble tea clothing and add-ons final 12 months and the journey has been great. With Printful handling the manufacturing, achievement and transport, I can attention on advertising and marketing and building my brand. I've related with boba fanatics everywhere in the world and these days reached 10,000 fans on Instagram. I'm just beginning my journey to earning extra passive earnings, however Shopify and Printful make it very easy, and I am very constructive!"

6. Developing A New App

By now, you've probably noticed a trend: growing stuff tends to cause passive profits. This is even more authentic inside the world of cellular software. If you're a developer or programmer, you might want to try creating apps as a passive profits flow.

You can cross approximately it in two methods. First, you can charge a charge for people who want to shop for your app. Second, you may make your app loose and monetize with ads. My fiance did this a few years in the past and nevertheless makes a side income from his app to this present day.

He offered code from Code Canyon. Then, he used a tool referred to as Eclipse and mounted the Android development SDK to make changes to the code to create his personal specific app. You can monetize an app in a number of methods, consisting of jogging in-app marketing, presenting pay walled content, and charging for top rate capabilities.

7. Adventure Into Stocks

When reading the income resources of the sector's richest people, it's quite secure to mention that shares have played a massive function in their deep, endless bank money owed.

While the act of investing in shares is quite passive, the research that is going into it's miles active. Warren Buffett reads 500 pages a day, however he's not analyzing your common thriller ebook. Nope. He reads enterprise's annual reviews. By doing this he better is aware whether or no longer a commercial enterprise is performing nicely, which facilitates him enhance his capacity to spend money on shares.

Stock investments assist you to earn passive income that stretches a ways beyond what your fee at your nine-to-5 job is really worth. So, recall this passive earnings idea if you're updated on various markets and enterprise moves.

8. Buy and sell properties

Depending on in which and whilst you buy, real property may be an awesome manner to make passive profits. In famous cities like Dubai, housing costs had been projected to upward thrust by means of an outstanding 12% to twenty% compared to the average fees from the preceding 12 months.

By purchasing pre-built condos, you could land some lower-value houses that'll growth in price by the point it's in the end constructed, permitting you to promote the assets for a income as soon as it's entire.

As with all investments, it can be volatile, so it's high-quality to speak with a real estate agent if you're new to the game that will help you buy the proper investment assets.

Shawn Breyer, proprietor of Breyer Home Buyers, shares: "My female friend, now spouse, graduated regulation college with $173,000 of college debt, and we set the period of the loan to be paid over 15 years, which made our month-to-month payments come out to be $1,459 per month. We wanted to apply apartment assets cash drift to cowl our monthly regulation college debt. Our first choice was to buy a duplex and stay on one side whilst we rented out the opposite aspect. This on my own stored us the $1,350 in housing charges that we had prior to shopping for the duplex.

"Instead of allocating that cash closer to greater essential bills on the faculty debt, we stored that money and purchased another duplex years later. This acquisition brought $650 in monthly cash go with the flow, which we snowballed into a 3rd assets. The three houses furnished us with a further $2,500 per month in savings and profits that we were capable of then placed towards extra primary payments. The splendor of this method is that our tenants are paying down our regulation school debt and if we have been to lose our jobs or have a scientific emergency, then we will depend totally on the rental income to pay for the college debt for us."

9. Rent out your spare room

If you've got a further room in your rental, you could lease it to someone for a selected period. Platforms like Airbnb will join you with individuals who are seeking out their next gateway. Airbnbs are favored due to the fact they're generally inexpensive than inns, that means you can make a higher passive earnings by list your loose area on Airbnb.

It's really worth noting that becoming an Airbnb host requires work upfront. You might ought to renovate or provide your room before list it on the marketplace. To make it definitely passive, you may rent a element-time property manager to create listings and look after your properties. Keep in thoughts, though, that they'll price a monthly fee between eight% and 10% of the month-to-month rent gathered.

Martin Dasko, founding father of Studenomics, makes passive earnings renting his apartment on Airbnb. He explains, "I determined to present Airbnb a shot after I stayed in a single on a visit to NYC. I cherished the idea and desired to get in on it. I positioned my condominium up for rent and become amazed by the call for. I turned into able to charge $169/night time in downtown Toronto. My biggest win came while a corporation contacted me because they had been sending some personnel to Toronto.

"They booked the unit for the whole month. I didn't should fear about locating new guests. The splendor of Airbnb is that you may turn it on and rancid as you please. When you're seeking to make a few extra cash, you may put your area up for hire. You can also hire out that spare bed room."

10. How To Become An affiliate marketer

Affiliate marketing is one of the satisfactory passive income opportunities available nowadays. The upside to it is that nearly each huge brand has an associate application, so you can promote some pretty popular merchandise and rake inside the dough.

The disadvantage is that you handiest make a fee at the sale. Shopify's associate application, for example, permits you to earn as much as $fifty eight in keeping with referral, that is a first rate income. Other on-line corporations best supply a measly $five to $10 in referral bonus.

So you'll need to make sure you do a little research into the great associate marketing programs before you get started. Blogging has a tendency to be the most cost-effective way to make ordinary associate commissions without having to spend money on ads.

Sireesha Narumanchi, founding father of Crowd Work News, shares, "I began my side hustle as a blogger a bit over two years ago, and this has been the maximum extraordinary adventure to this point. As a content creator, most of my profits is from associates, and it's completely passive. It wasn't clean to juggle my activity and commercial enterprise, however it was totally well worth it. I do put in lots of hours studying, crafting, and working on enterprise techniques, but as soon as my content material is executed, it generates profits passively time and again. The giant satisfaction of supporting humans and showing them that there is a preference of operating from home and earning a respectable income is my trophy at the quit of the day."

11 Market your videos For Sell

If you constantly find yourself in the midst of drama and excitement, you may want to drag out your cell phone and hit Record. Doing that will let you make a few passive earnings. The trendy video advertising stats indicate that human beings are enthusiastic about video content, so that you need to be capable of discover an target audience to your films.

Why? Because you may promote that video to a news website online. And if the video takes to the air, you can make a few ordinary money for weeks, months, and from time to time even years. Of path, the easiest way to get in on the motion is to be at public events such as protests, demonstrations, and festivals.

Wherever there's controversy, you'll discover possibilities on your content material to be bought. And if you're accurate at producing enjoyable content, agencies pays you to create viral motion pictures along side supplying a share of typical profits.

Peter Kock, proprietor of Seller at Heart, stocks how he made passive profits importing videos to famous websites: "I uploaded some films to Newsflare and Rumble. When my content material receives bought, 50% of all sales generated gets stressed to my non-public account. My motion pictures have been featured on MSN, AOL, Yahoo, Daily Mail, The Guardian, etc. With News flare, I revamped $4,000 up to now and nevertheless I'm getting royalties for films uploaded a few years in the past."

12. Buy and flip websites

Do you've got revel in of making ecommerce web sites? If so, you may make passive income constructing and promoting them.

You'll probably need to generate some revenue (to show that your save has ability). But if you've were given first rate layout competencies and might put up some content material on your internet site, you can promote it to a person looking to buy a pre-built ecommerce shop.

If you're seeking out a place to sell your internet site, you may strive out Shopify's Exchange marketplace. On the platform, you could sell your newly built online save or your superior six- or seven-discern shop. It's the precise platform for internet site flipping.

13. Ask for company stocks

Yup, your nine-to-5 process also can end up a passive income stream. No, it's not the hours you work. However, your business enterprise stocks or any organization-matching retirement plans permit you to rating a few quite first rate passive profits.

I honestly used this passive profits approach to pay for the down payment on my apartment. And it most effective took years. Of route, you'll probably need to make investments a number of your very own cash, however the greater bit that the company adds is a pleasing perk, in case you're willing to try it. (And believe me, few humans ever do.)

If you're beginning a new 9-to-five activity, make certain to invite for enterprise stocks as a part of your hiring package. You'll thank me later.

14. Adventure Into You Tube channel

YouTube is the passive income move that just continues on giving. From backed films to advert sales, you'll find that you may make habitual profits from your YouTube channel.

The secret to developing a successful YouTube channel is creating content material on a consistent agenda for a long time. Make positive each video you add is well made and something human beings want. If you stick with it for the lengthy haul, you'll eventually start reaping the passive earnings rewards.

Already have a YouTube channel? Check out our article How to Make Money on YouTube for ideas on a way to monetize your video content.

Matthew Ross, co-proprietor and COO Slumber Yard, started out his passive profits journey on YouTube: "Back in 2013, my commercial enterprise partner and I were extremely interested by wearable generation—Garmin watches, Fitbit pastime trackers, and so on.—and decided to start a YouTube channel that might overview those varieties of products. We certainly just loved checking out out the watches and thought we could earn a touch marketing cash at the facet.

"In total, we invested approximately $5,000 creating the channel and buying the goods to review. However, around that point, the wearable technology class exploded and we started making extra cash than we ever imagined. Needless to mention, I controlled to turn my hobby into a business. We've been able to grow pinnacle-line sales to over $2.Five million, we've employed 10 full-time employees, and we currently moved the enterprise's headquarters to a brand new contemporary 7,000-square-foot office in Reno, Nevada. Today, our websites and YouTube channels appeal to over four million site visitors consistent with month, blended."

15. Market your images Online

While being a photographer may seem like an active income business, it's tritely no longer. Photographers don't most effective make cash from taking pix. They sell them too. Stock photograph sites, magazines, and canvas printing on your clients are a number of the methods you could make massive greenbacks inside the images space.

All you need to get started is a brilliant digicam. But nowadays, you may even use your phone to seize amazing images. Consider taking outstanding images and listing them on inventory images sites to earn earnings within the form of royalties.

Jacob Hakobyan makes passive income together with his photography enterprise, Shot life Studio. He shares, "Having profound enterprise schooling and what some can also bear in mind as very stable office jobs, we felt that we had the capacity to do more. Not financially, but spiritually. As a brother-sister-husband trio, we started Shot life Studio really due to the fact all of us had a common love for images, and there was an delivered thrill of leading a enterprise of our very own. With our CPA know-how coming to useful resource, we organized a clear approach at the boom of the business and managed to double our profits from 12 months to year, attaining a five-parent facet income."

16. Assist groups convey in customers

Are you a savvy marketer or salesclerk? If so, there are heaps of agencies a good way to pay you referral charges for bringing more customers to them.

For instance, DJs, photographers, and different solopreneurs are usually seeking to develop their client base. If you control to find clients that signal a protracted-time period contract, they'll thankfully pay you a referral bonus.

So if you are desirable at networking, you could begin constructing a passive income via your connections. All it takes to get this enterprise started is a couple of emails or messages.

17. Write And Publish Ebook

Ebooks exploded onto the scene round 2010 and are nevertheless a hugely popular content material medium. Anyone with expert knowledge in a specific problem can write an e-book to percentage their thoughts with the world. You ought not to move at it by myself. Platforms like Upwork make it clean to locate ebook writers and editors who can help with the manner.

You'll want to publish your manuscript via Amazon Kindle to make it to be had to your audience. Some advertising is also required to get the word out to as many human beings as feasible. Once you destroy into the e-book space, it's viable to create passive income through web page reads and Kindle sales, that is how most ebook writers make cash.

Allie McCormick makes passive income by using growing eBooks. She explains, "In 2016, once I became pregnant with my son, I commenced an Amazon Kindle publishing side hustle to with a bit of luck earn just $500 in keeping with month by the time he changed into born so I could avoid going lower back to the workplace. While I didn't give up working right away, 18 months later, I had a six-discern passive profits commercial enterprise that enabled me to do so. Biggest win? This enterprise nevertheless runs totally on autopilot to at the moment. I work on it one to 2 hours weekly and take three to 4 weeks off at a time while nevertheless raking within the dough!"

18. Sell your undesirable stuff

Looking to follow Marie Kondo's recommendation and start decluttering your home? Well, you may need to turn that clutter into cold, tough cash.

We all have the ones piles of bins packed with stuff we haven't concept about in years. You can either maintain onto it for a hazard to end up on an episode of Hoarders or you may sell it online to help you make passive income. You might have to dig deep, but you may discover you've got some gadgets which are well worth a few critical cash.

So in case you don't understand wherein to start with regards to passive profits, your closet might be your fine bet.

19. Develop and Market virtual merchandise Online

Digital products are media assets human beings can't contact physically. They typically encompass downloadable documents such as audio books, PDFs, templates, or plug-ins.

Digital merchandise have excessive income margins because no stock or storage expenses are incurred. You simplest have to make the asset once and you can promote it again and again. There's no restrict on the range of copies you may promote.

You can create a Shopify save to sell your digital merchandise online. Selling those products is the epitome of passive earnings, because the entire process may be automated on Shopify with instantaneous downloads.

Kelan and Brittany Kline, the duo at the back of The Savvy Couple, tell us, "Last month, we released a Shopify save with a few digital merchandise to promote to our readers. Specifically, we made the Budgeting Binder to help humans learn how to organize their budget and start to finances. Since the release, our shop has made us over $1,500 in income and maintains to grow every week. Since all of our merchandise are virtual, this profits is completely passive. As long as we maintain to funnel readers to our shop, we retain to get income."

20. Use passive earnings apps

Passive earnings apps work precisely as they sound— you install them on your telephone and perform some moves to earn cash. The movements can range from doing ordinary sports, along with watching motion pictures to turning a small monetary investment right into a passive income circulation. There are masses of apps to start putting your cellular device and time to better use. Here are a few top ones:

* Fundrise. Fundrise lets you put money into actual property tasks with an initial minimal funding of $1,000. It comes with the choice to take quarterly dividends, which serve as your passive profits.

* InboxDollars. InboxDollars offers cashback for doing sports that you're probable to do besides, inclusive of buying, watching TV, and searching the net. The cashback and the $five bonus for signing up are your passive earnings.

* Dosh. gives you the option to hyperlink your debit and credit score playing cards to its system. When you pay for something using these playing cards, you earn passive earnings within the form of cashback.

21. Develop and license audio tracks

If you've got a few audio abilties, why no longer placed them to work? Making audio tracks for different human beings's use is a superb way to earn extra money, as humans are constantly seeking to logo themselves with the proper sound.

You can license your tracks out on platforms like Sound Cloud and Audio socket if you want to create full songs and earn a few passive earnings via royalties. All you need to do is research your target audience and discover what kind of content material is trending. From there, you could quick start building your portfolio of tunes. You by no means recognize—it might transform into something larger.

If you find a passion for creating audio, you can test with a extensive variety of different merchandise, from intros and outros to full albums and mixing samples. Alternatively, your audio tune may be as simple as a jingle or a podcast intro.

22. Make Money from your unused area

Space is a treasured commodity that maximum of us don't have enough of. Whether you're presently only the usage of your storage room part-time or having greater space in your home, there are tons of methods to create some greater profits with that unused area. For example, you could lease out garage areas on websites like Neighbor.Com, so people have an extra region to keep their property.

If you have got room in your garage or even a further parking space, you can lease these out simultaneously. If you're booking a area for an event and also you don't need it all the time, you may check out web sites like Share My Space, wherein you may advertise your to be had square photos to all people who wishes it.

Alternatively, you may offer employees and experts without an office a exceptional place to work comfortably. This manner, you'll earn passive earnings while the renters get a comfortable work environment. It's win-win!

23. Develop a process board/Website

A process board is a website used by employers to promote task vacancies to humans. People can observe for vacant roles remotely with some clicks. You can fee organizations to submit to your board, and up sell features like unlimited get entry to for your expertise pool to boom your income.

You can both design a activity board from scratch or buy a premade topic and start there. The bulk of your effort need to be devoted to growing focus on your activity board. You can write a press release, put up on social media, and run paid commercials to get traction early.

Once you build a solid customers of ordinary, straightforward clients, you could anticipate a big a part of your profits to be passive. Check out web sites like Dribble or Prolonger for idea.

Strengthen your economic future with those passive income ideas

Passive income can definitely help elevate your income and fill within the gaps that your nine-to-five activity can't fill on its personal. If you're trying to create an extra income movement so that you can strengthen your economic destiny, the ideas in this list assist you to do this.

And it's OK if you want your full-time gig too. The work that is going into incomes passive profits tends to be manageable when paired with a 9-to-5. So, yup, you could do each.